SHARON FELICIA ACHEAMPONG

WHAT IS YOUR TREASURE?

COVER PHOTOGRAPHY BY JOSH ALBA

MODEL – TICHAKUNDA GABI

ISBN: 978-1-67816-187-3

DEDICATION:

For Tichakunda Gabi & Josh Alba,

Thank you for inspiring this collection. May you always be adventurous, curious and happy.

Xoxo

Sharon

SHARON FELICIA ACHEAMPONG

WHAT IS YOUR TREASURE?

COVER PHOTOGRAPHY BY JOSH ALBA

MODEL – TICHAKUNDA GABI

SFA – WHAT IS YOUR TREASURE?

CONTENTS:

- ➢ Present ...11
- ➢ Son of Helios ...13
- ➢ A Letter From Aphrodite ...15
- ➢ Sols Tears ...17
- ➢ Bleeding Veins ...19
- ➢ Inferno ...21
- ➢ Riversong ...23
- ➢ Thrillseeker ...25
- ➢ A Toast ...28
- ➢ What Is Your Treasure? ...30

PRESENT

Present,

It's a gift,

Open it!

It's a brand new day,

Live it, make it count.

Make it special, make it memorable.

Present,

You're so lucky,

Open it!

It's a brand new opportunity,

Take advantage of it, use it well.

Make it the most exceptional day, you've lived today.

Present,

How exciting,

Open it!

It's a brand new adventure,

Yours to explore, yours to experience.

Make memories and enjoy the ride.

SON OF HELIOS

With each new day I rise,

The sun heralds a new beginning.

I am the son of the sun,

I take heed of the call.

The call to a brand new battle,

The call to a brand new conquest.

Yesterday is gone,

Left behind are the memories.

Fuelled by the golden rays,

And inspired by the past to do better.

I shall climb higher today,

I shall go further than yesterday.

A setback I not a failure,

Neither is it even a setback.

It is a detour, a diversion.

An extra chapter in this adventure series,

Another learning curve for extra credits,

Credits all leading up to the end goal.

With each new day I rise,

The sun heralds a new beginning.

I am a son of the sun,

And today I shall shine brighter,

Way brighter than I did yesterday.

Because all I do is shine.

A LETTER FROM APHRODITE

Take a moment, stop, and breathe,

I am right here, so close, so near.

Not out there in those artificial creations,

Those monstrosities they call art.

Take a moment, shut them all out.

Listen, listen to your heart.

For that's where I am,

Where I've always been.

You don't need a map from the outside,

Your guiding light is within you.

All the love, all the beauty is right here.

Your job is to open up and let it out.

For it is only by sharing it,

That you can multiply it.

You have it because you are worth it,

You are lovely,

You are beautiful.

Humanity did not create you, the universe did.

They cannot label you,

They do not own you.

You're a gift,

Priceless, Precious, Perfect.

You're a jewel,

Rare, Radiant, Real.

SOLS TEARS

They give me a bad reputation,

They are humans, I shouldn't be surprised.

They love me, and then they hate me.

It's a mish mash of emotions.

A cesspool of indecision.

They are humans, I shouldn't be surprised.

Have they seen how bright everything becomes,

Whenever I am around?

I literally light up the room, when I show up.

The colours pop, there is energy in the air.

And how they glow, sun kissed they call it,

Whenever I touch their skin.

But they give me a bad reputation,

They are humans, I shouldn't be surprised.

So they admire me in secret,

Not coming close enough to touch.

I see the longing in their eyes,

Hear the yearning in their hearts.

But that's all it amounts to,

A longing and a yearning from afar.

So I hang out with those who will have me,

Those who bloom under my touch,

Those who bask in my glow,

Those who celebrate my arrival,

With a song and maybe a dance.

BLEEDING VEINS

The irony of it all,

It baffles me,

I'm yet to understand, I doubt I will.

The effort of it all,

Wasted in one fell swoop.

Is there, was there,

What are you talking about?

The painstaking effort,

What was it all for then,

If this is how it is going to end?

The love, I know now it wasn't.

Just calculating sneakiness,

Veiled as the kindness we all crave.

I gave you life!

Yes I stand tall & claim that boldly.

Yet you destroy me without a second thought.

It would at least be better,

If you were to replace me with,

Something better, I wouldn't be so hurt.

But of course you aren't,

Why am I not surprised?

You had it all with me,

Love, food, shelter.

But no, you'd rather have death traps,

All decked out and jewelled,

But in truth all they are,

Are prisons with golden bars.

INFERNO

The burn, the power, the savagery,

Nothing calls anything to action,

The way an inferno does.

You see it, but you cannot touch it.

It wields its power,

In a dimension unfamiliar to you.

Powered by the air, but not air.

Given a veil of invisibility,

Yet being very much visible.

The inferno, you feel it,

You feel it and you dare not ignore it.

Harnessed it is power,

Power unlike you've ever seen,

Power unlike you've ever known.

Power which even when harnessed cannot be tamed.

As an enemy it is deadly,

A foe you'd rather not make.

A foe with a rapid ability,

To recreate, morph, and attack again.

Nature's version, of a cloning machine.

One ice cube does not create an iceberg,

One drop does not create the ocean,

But a single flicker...yes just one.

RIVERSONG

My voice, hear my voice,

Attune yourself to my mood,

Pick up on all the nuances.

The slight lisps,

The breaks in the dry lands,

The resurrections in the oasis's.

My voice, hear my voice.

It is my song, a song of the ages.

A song of life, love, loss.

A song of time, wear and tear.

A song of paths carved out,

In places I was told I couldn't go.

They placed rocks before me.

All in an attempt to stop me.

For in appearance, I am weaker.

But I make up for that in persistence.

Each day pushing a little more,

Each effort building up to the total.

My voice, hear my voice,

It is a battle cry,

A song of victory, a song of overcoming.

I began as a stream, insignificant, unimportant.

But look at me now, crested waves loud and proud.

I am now the sea do you see?

THRILL SEEKER

Why?

But then why not?

Again why not?

There is danger you say,

There's always been danger I say.

Why go look for it you say,

That's not entirely true I say.

Life is but a book, waiting to be read,

The earth a treasure map,

Waiting to be deciphered.

The people, friends waiting to be made.

And who knows, maybe an enemy or two.

Danger is not always danger,

Sometimes it is just a term,

A tern we use to label the unknown.

What we don't know scares us,

How about we get to know it?

Un-danger it if you want to call it that,

Take the sting out of the bee.

What are we if we are not alive?

How can we be alive if we do not live?

How can we be alive, residing in prisons?

Prisons of our minds,

Prisons created by our imagination.

There is so much truth out there,

Truth waiting to be discovered,

Truth waiting to be learnt,

Truth waiting to be shared.

It certainly won't come to us,

So here goes nothing,

After it we go.

Why?

Why not?

Why not now, rather than later?

Later when all we can say is why?

Because then it would be too late,

To go out and seek the answers.

So here's the chance,

Here's to another one,

Another adventure,

Another memory in the bag,

And hey,

Why not...

A TOAST

A toast to friends, friendship,

A toast to those we know and those unknown.

A toast to those here and those there,

The ones we met, the ones we left,

The ones we shall meet,

And maybe meet again.

A toast to persons, personalities,

A toast to traits, characters, habits.

A toast to differences, which we all bring to the table.

The spices which lend their distinct aroma,

To this brew called life.

Cheers and cheers again.

A toast to memories, adventures,

A toast to paths travelled, bridges crossed.

A toast to fears conquered in pursuit of the unknown.

The days gone by that we shall treasure,

For the smiles they bring each time we remember.

And the knowledge that we shall make more, we shall
smile again.

WHAT IS YOUR TREASURE?

I met an old man once,

I ought to rephrase that to wise,

For old seems quite unfitting.

Not to say he was young,

But that's not the point.

He had a look in his eyes,

The kind that has seen it all.

He had an aura about him,

The kind that says I am at peace with it all.

He asked me a question,

It seemed easy enough,

If we are to judge by my prompt response.

"What is your treasure?"

Of course I knew what my treasure was,

I had been working for years you see,

To create the so called nest egg.

When I retired, sometime in the future,

I would not be haunted by sleepless nights.

Spent worrying about the financial wellbeing,

Of my family and I.

He shook his head,

A smile playing on his lips.

He looked out in the distance,

Eyes fixed on something only he saw.

"The thing with money," he began,

And already I had a feeling,

Of where this conversation was headed.

"It is affected so easily, by wars, depressions, recessions,
and the good old fraud."

"One day you have it,

Next day you don't."

He made a lot of sense,

Sense I knew deep down,

But refused to acknowledge.

I had no comeback to that,

Other than a deflated "oh"

He looked at me,

Smile still on his lips.

And again he asked the same question.

"What is your treasure?"

I had already given my answer,

But he clearly expected another one.

I had nothing to lose,

Time was on my side.

So I tried again.

This time I left the money out.

I had amassed quite a number of properties to date,

If not money,

At least we would have a roof over our heads.

He tilted his head slightly to the side,

He reminded me of my dog,

When I'd just given an instruction,

Which he couldn't completely comprehend.

He shook his head,

As if to shake everything back into place.

This time he didn't look into the distance.

I guess this was a response,

That required some face to face action.

"A flood, an earthquake, a natural disaster,

Or something as small and insignificant,

As a lit match in the wrong place."

I saw the end of his response,

Way before he finished speaking.

"Could leave you with nothing,

Other than the clothes on your back."

I was starting to feel deflated,

And a tad bit irritated.

Here was a complete stranger,

Making mincemeat, out of my great big plan.

And even more irritating was the fact,

That he was right, & I couldn't argue with him.

Except question myself,

"Was I then slaving away for nothing?"

He sensed my despondency,
And he chuckled, I could have cursed,
Laughing at my misery!
But I was raised better.
So I sighed, and he sighed too,
What did he have to sigh about?
He had all the answers.
He looked at the ground for a while,
I followed his gaze,
He had very nice shoes.
They reminded me of my brother.
There was a standing joke in my family,
That he knew more about shoes and fashion,
Than all the women in our clan combined.
I smiled at the memory.
Realizing with a tinge of regret,
How I had not spoken to him in a while.
I really should call him.

Maybe meet up for drinks or something.

A light cough woke me from my reverie,

I knew somehow that the question,

Yes, same question was making a comeback.

Two minutes earlier I would have,

In all honesty, just politely excused myself.

But I was ready now,

The way one is for an exam,

That they have studied for, for so long,

Failing would be an absolute impossibility.

And it seemed he knew too,

There was something different,

In the way he asked.

I just could not put my finger on it.

Same question, same words,

But it was different, I had been enlightened.

Though that glow of enlightenment was,

To fade as quickly as it had arrived.

Away with the material trappings,

This time I went with family and friends.

And not because I wanted a different answer,

But because in that moment I realized,

They were something no one could take away.

He nodded then almost under his breath he added,
"There is always death..."

I felt like a balloon,

That had just collided with a pin.

This conversation was going nowhere,

Or maybe it was,

I wasn't giving up without a fight,

Or a challenge or a comeback,

Or whatever it is you want to call it.

"But the memories don't die,"

Yes, that was my counter attack.

Even the way I said it,

Had a trace of a challenge.

A take that if you can undertone.

He smiled, nodded again and gave a soundless clap.

"Memories, yes no one can steal those."

I could feel myself swell up,

Proud moment it was.

"But you have to make them first," he added, looking
at me directly.

And for some reason, that made me squirm.

"Once the money is gone, memories of it of it won't do
much for you.

Memories of experiences however,

Can breathe life into a dead day."

Deep down I knew I needed,

More experience making and less money making.

And it had taken a random stranger at a bus stop,

To make me consciously aware of that.

I realized I had been looking at the ground,

Shamefaced indeed I was.

I looked up; I had to at least thank him.

But suddenly I was standing alone.

He was no longer next to me.

Nor was he walking away in either direction.

It was as if he had just vanished into thin air.

The possibility ought to have scared me.

But I was strangely at peace,

Whoever or whatever he was or had been,

He had helped me create an experience,

That marked my soul forever.

SFA – WHAT IS YOUR TREASURE?

SFA – WHAT IS YOUR TREASURE?

www.ingramcontent.com/pod-product-compliance
Lightning Source LLC
Chambersburg PA
CBHW030311030426
42337CB00012B/670